Pirate School
Nice Dog!

Adapted from Pirate School: Where's That Dog?
by Jeremy Strong

Illustrated by Ian Cunliffe

Adapted by Maureen Haselhurst

Published by Pearson Education Limited, Edinburgh Gate, Harlow, Essex, CM20 2JE
Registered company number: 872828

www.pearsonschools.co.uk

Adapted text based on *Pirate School: Where's That Dog?*, originally published by Puffin Books Ltd in 2004.

Text copyright © Jeremy Strong, 2004
Illustrations copyright © Ian Cunliffe, 2004
All rights reserved.
Cover design by Bigtop

Adaptation by Maureen Haselhurst

Cover/interior illustrations and text all used by kind permission of Puffin Books Ltd.

The moral rights of the author and illustrator have been asserted.

First published 2012

16 15 14 13
10 9 8 7 6 5 4 3

British Library Cataloguing in Publication Data
A catalogue record for this book is available from the British Library

ISBN 978 0 435 07609 2

Copyright notice
All rights reserved. No part of this publication may be reproduced in any form or by any means (including photocopying or storing it in any medium by electronic means and whether or not transiently or incidentally to some other use of this publication) without the written permission of the copyright owner, except in accordance with the provisions of the Copyright, Designs and Patents Act 1988 or under the terms of a licence issued by the Copyright Licensing Agency, Saffron House, 6–10 Kirby Street, London EC1N 8TS (www.cla.co.uk). Applications for the copyright owner's written permission should be addressed to the publisher.

Printed and bound in Malaysia (CTP-VP)

Acknowledgements
We would like to thank the children and teachers of Bangor Central Integrated Primary School, NI; Barley Hill School, Thame; Bishop Henderson C of E Primary School, Somerset; Brookside Community Primary School, Somerset; Catcott Primary School, Somerset; Cheddington Combined School, Buckinghamshire; Cofton Primary School, Birmingham; Dair House Independent School, Buckinghamshire; Deal Parochial School, Kent; Lawthorn Primary School, North Ayrshire; Newbold Riverside Primary School, Rugby and Windmill Primary School, Oxford for their invaluable help in the development and trialling of the Bug Club resources.

Every effort has been made to contact copyright holders of material reproduced in this book. Any omissions will be rectified in subsequent printings if notice is given to the publisher.

Contents

Chapter 1
Bad News 4

Chapter 2
The Inspection Begins...................... 9

Chapter 3
A Hop and a Skip and – Oh Dear!.... 15

Chapter 4
Jazz to the Rescue 18

Chapter 5
The Chase Begins 24

Chapter 6
Ten Out of Ten at Last!................... 31

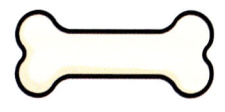

Chapter 1
Bad News

Would you like to go to Pirate School? If you ever met the head teacher, you probably wouldn't. Think of a monster with a fiery ginger wig. Now give her big, grabby hands and a wooden leg. Put the monster in a mini pirate ship on wheels, complete with cannons. That's the head teacher, Patagonia Clatterbottom.

"Hurry up and answer the door, Snitty!" yelled Patagonia, who was in a very shouty mood that particular morning.

The school secretary dashed out of the bathroom with her dress tucked into her tights. She opened the door and there was the postman with a **VERY IMPORTANT** letter. He also had a dog clinging to his leg.

"She's a stray," said the postman. "I can't seem to shake her off!"

"We'll look after her," smiled Flo.

"Oh no, we won't!" roared Mrs Clatterbottom, and she slammed the door in the postman's face.

"I wish we could have looked after the dog," said Flo.

"We can!" laughed Smudge. "I've smuggled her aboard the ship. She's under my jumper!"

"Let's call her Jazz," suggested Ziggy.
"We'll have to hide her," said Corkella.

There was a terrible roar from Mrs Clatterbottom's cabin.

"Aargh! This letter says that we're going to be inspected! I hate inspections and I hate inspectors! They'll close down the school if we don't get a good mark. Aargh!"

Chapter 2
The Inspection Begins

Two pirate inspectors arrived the next day. Miss Piefinger was as big as a rhinoceros. She wore an eyepatch with a hole cut in it so that she could see out. Mr Crankle had a wooden leg and a face like a toad. He had two spare legs that he threw at people when he got cross.

Patagonia introduced her staff.

"Mad Maggott teaches walking the gangplank. Mrs Muggwump teaches rope-swinging and Miss Fishgripp is our capturing-skills expert."

Miss Piefinger sniffed loudly. "Who teaches sailing?"

"I do," fibbed Patagonia, who was actually a useless sailor.

Just then, there was a loud bark.

"Dogs aren't allowed in school," grunted Mr Crankle.

"My ship is dog-less!" roared Mrs Clatterbottom.

"Ruff!" went Ziggy. "It was me. Just my little joke."

"Let's make a start," growled Mr Crankle. "We'll watch rope-swinging first. That boy there, get on the rope." He pointed his knobbly finger at Smudge.

Smudge hated rope-swinging. It was like hanging on to a twisting snake. He groaned as he grabbed hold of the rope.

"Climb higher!" snapped Mrs Muggwump, poking him with a stick. "Now swing!"

Smudge swung out over the water and then came swooshing back.

"Duck!" shouted Corkella.

Too late. Smudge hurtled through the air and crashed into Mr Crankle, who tumbled overboard.

Miss Piefinger sniffed. "Marks out of ten for rope-swinging – zero."

Patagonia was furious with Smudge. "Zero out of ten? You piffling little pirate!"

"Ruff! Ruff!" growled Jazz.

"Ruff! Ruff!" repeated Corkella. "It was me this time. Ruff!"

"Well, be quiet and haul Mr Crankle back on board," roared Mrs Clatterbottom.

Chapter 3
A Hop and a Skip and – Oh Dear!

"Capturing-skills next," ordered the soggy Mr Crankle.

"Ziggy will try to capture Flo, but she must stop him," explained Miss Fishgripp. "Begin!"

Ziggy began to chase Flo around the deck, but she ducked and dived out of his reach and hid behind Miss Piefinger.

Ziggy grabbed at Flo, but instead he collided with Miss Piefinger's rhinoceros-sized knees.

"Niggling kneecaps!" groaned Miss Piefinger as she crashed into Miss Snitty, who tumbled into Patagonia's boat-pram.

All three of them hurtled backwards and tumbled down into the hold.

Mr Crankle got out his notebook. "Marks out of ten for capturing-skills – zero."

"Ruff!" went Jazz, who thought this was a great game.

"There is a dog on board!" yelled Miss Piefinger.

"Ruff! Ruff! Ruff!" chorused Corkella, Ziggy, Smudge and Flo. "It was us! Ruff!"

Chapter 4
Jazz to the Rescue

The inspection was not going well. "Let's see how you do on the gangplank!" said the inspectors.

"Get on with it, you landlubbers!" Mad Maggot bellowed at the children. "Walk the plank!"

"He always makes us jump off the gangplank," grumbled Ziggy. "Well, I'm not going to jump this time."

"Nor are we," said the others, lining up behind him.

"Jump!" bellowed Mad Maggott.

"Shan't!" shouted Ziggy bravely.

It's a mutiny!

"Do something, Maggott!" roared Mrs Clatterbottom.

Mad Maggott was too scared to go out very far himself, so he began leaping up and down, trying to make the children jump.

The gangplank catapulted them into the air, but they bounced back onto it with a BOYOIINNGG!!!

Mad Maggott made one last enormous leap and came crashing back down. Up into the air went the children.

"Help!" they shouted.

"Ruff!"

Suddenly, up popped Jazz from the crow's nest. She grabbed Ziggy's leg. Ziggy held onto Corkella's arm. Flo held on to Corkella's hand and Smudge held on to Flo's leg.

"THERE IS A DOG!" bellowed the inspectors. The furious Mr Crankle threw one of his spare legs at Jazz. She thought it was a stick and went to catch it. Oops! She dropped the children and down they fell.

"Waaaaaah!"

POOOMMFFFFF!!!

They landed on top of Miss Piefinger. The squashed inspector waved her notebook from beneath the pile of children.

"Marks out of ten for the gangplank – zero."

Mr Crankle snarled at Mrs Clatterbottom. "Tomorrow is your last chance. You'll need to get top marks for sailing or we'll close the school down. And get rid of that dog!"

Chapter 5
The Chase Begins

That night Patagonia Clatterbottom couldn't sleep. "I'm hopeless at sailing," she thought miserably. "We're going to fail the last test and it will be all my fault."

All the children knew that Patagonia was a useless sailor, but Pirate School was fun and no one wanted it to close.

"We've got to do something," said Corkella.

Smudge had an idea.

"We could escape. We could sail the ship away. I've got a plan …"

Early next morning, the children hauled up the anchor and let down the sails. Corkella took the wheel, but as she steered the ship out of the harbour they heard a shout.

"Stop that school! It's escaping!"

The furious inspectors clambered into their ship and gave chase.

"They're catching up," warned Flo.

"Load the cannons!" ordered Ziggy. "When I shout 'Hard about!' head back towards the inspectors."

Smudge and Flo loaded the cannons and soon they were speeding back towards the inspectors' ship with the wind filling their sails.

"Fire!" yelled Ziggy.

BOOM!

It was a direct hit! The inspectors' ship was riddled with holes and drifted to a halt.

"Boarding party!" cried Smudge, and the four children swung across onto the enemy ship.

A boarding party! I love parties!

The inspectors made a grab for them, but the children escaped their clutches.

"Take them prisoner," ordered Flo. The astonished inspectors found themselves being bundled back on board the pirate ship. Jazz trotted over and tugged at Mr Crankle's shoelaces.

"We told you to get rid of that dog!" shouted Miss Piefinger. "Throw it overboard at once!"

Ziggy scowled. "All right – you've asked for it!" he hissed. "Walk the plank – both of you!"

SPLISH! went Crankle.

SPLASH! went Piefinger.

SPLOSH! went Jazz, who loved getting wet.

By the time Patagonia Clatterbottom woke up it was all over. She stared in horror at the inspectors struggling through the waves.

"Pants and double pants!" she howled. "Those kids have really got us into trouble now. Waahhhhh!"

Chapter 6
Ten Out of Ten at Last!

Miss Piefinger coughed and spluttered as she pulled out her notebook.

"That was more like it!" she called. "Marks out of ten for sailing – ten! I have never seen such perfect displays of rope-swinging, capturing-skills and proper use of the gangplank."

"I agree," choked Mr Crankle as he sank under the water.

Jazz dived under and hauled him back.

"Nice dog," spluttered Crankle, as Jazz towed him back to the pirate boat.

"Very nice dog," agreed Piefinger, as Jazz went back for her.

So everyone was happy. The inspectors gave the school a terrific report and Mrs Clatterbottom threw a massive party.

That night Jazz crept from one person to another, giving everyone a good night lick – including Patagonia Clatterbottom.

"Nice dog," she grunted, and promptly fell asleep.